DO YOU COPY?

Birdseye's truck has a CB radio. People who use CB radios have their own lingo. They often use common words in a different way.

Some CB lingo:

copy verb—to understand, to hear what someone tells you on the radio	**handle** noun—the name people use to identify themselves on CB radio
eyeball verb—to look at	**patch** noun—city or town

Read the pairs of sentences that Birdseye wrote. In the blank, tell whether the underlined word is used as a noun or a verb. Then circle the sentence where Birdseye used the word as CB lingo.

_____ I don't know how to handle my truck very well.
_____ Say, good buddy, my handle is Turkey Feathers.

_____ Come in, Rainbow Robin. Do you copy me?
_____ I need a copy of a good CB dictionary.

_____ I'm heading for the next patch down the road.
_____ Soon I'm going to have to patch that old tire.

_____ My eyeballs are tired from driving too long.
_____ I want to stop and eyeball the pretty view.

Grammar and Usage Workbook

YOU WRITE THE STORY — PART 1

Natasha is making up a story for her little brother. You can help by thinking up some good nouns for the story. They can be as silly or as wild as you want. Write them in the blanks below. Then use them to finish Natasha's story on page 5.

1. _____
   any common noun, singular

2. _____
   any proper noun

3. _____
   a day of the week, plural

4. _____
   any common noun, plural

5. _____
   any common noun, plural

6. _____
   a town, city, state, or country

7. _____
   an animal, singular

8. _____
   a piece of furniture, plural

9. _____
   an item of clothing, singular

10. _____
    an occupation, singular

11. _____
    any common noun, plural

12. _____
    a container, singular

13. _____
    a plant, plural

14. _____
    a noise, singular

15. _____
    any common noun, plural

16. _____
    any common noun, singular

17. _____
    something in a city, singular

18. _____
    a month, singular

Grammar and Usage Workbook

A TRUCK FULL OF WORDS

ABBREVIATIONS
noun = n.
verb = v.
adjective = adj.
adverb = adv.
pronoun = pron.
preposition = prep.
conjunction = conj.

Use a dictionary to find out the part of speech of the words below. Write the abbreviation after each word.

1. learn _____   2. them _____   3. itself _____
   curly _____   with _____   things _____

4. music _____   5. frog _____   6. because _____   7. tricky _____
   among _____   know _____   already _____   nearly _____

8. fresh _____   9. sister _____ 10. where _____   11. toward _____
   marry _____   anyone _____   enter _____   belong _____

Then fill in the puzzle. Choose the word from each pair above that matches the part of speech shown in the numbered box. Fill in all the words going down.

When you have finished, read across to see what I am carrying in my truck.

Grammar and Usage Workbook

ANYTHING BUT THAT!

Birdseye thinks it would be fun to be a chicken, or a swan, or an eagle. It might even be fun to be a robin or a pigeon. But she would NOT like to be an emperor penguin. Why? Here's how to find out:

Look in a dictionary to find the part of speech of each word below. Circle the word in each pair that can be both a noun and a verb.

1. taste
   wheat
2. rotate
   help
3. owl
   end
4. multiply
   yell
5. escape
   crumble
6. explain
   attack
7. toast
   grass
8. lose
   shine
9. heart
   quake
10. pretend
    urge
11. triangle
    interest
12. napkin
    drive

Write the first letter of each circled word in the blanks to find out why Birdseye doesn't want to be a penguin.

It's not the icy cold that I mind...

___ ___ ___ ___   ___ ___ ___   ___ ___ ___ ___ ___
1   2   3   4   5   6   7   8   9   10   11   12

2 Grammar and Usage Workbook

YOU WRITE THE STORY — PART 2

Fill in the blanks with nouns from page 4. The number tells you which word to use.

Once upon a time there was a fuzzy (1) _____ named (2) _____ . He liked to think he was fierce, but really he was only mean on (3) _____ , when he tore up (4) _____ and stomped on (5) _____ .

He lived in a cave in the middle of (6) _____ with his pet (7) _____ and five (8) _____ . He usually wore an orange (9) _____ . He was a (10) _____ , but he was also a collector of (11) _____ . He saved them in a (12) _____ .

One day, he was walking in (13) _____ that grew higher than his head when he heard a loud (14) _____ . There before him stood the awful giant (15) _____ .

(2) _____ dropped his (16) _____ and ran, but it was too late. The (15) _____ grabbed him and ate him in two mouthfuls.

The people in (6) _____ named a (17) _____ in his honor. They celebrate (2) _____ 's day every year on the 17th of (18) _____ .

Now draw a picture of the (1) _____ in your story.

Grammar and Usage Workbook 5

PAST, PRESENT, FUTURE

Birdseye is traveling in Africa. Below are some of the things she did, is doing, and will do while she is there. Write the correct form of the verb in the blanks—past, present, or future. Then draw her route on the map.

PAST

First I _____ (go) to Egypt. There I _____ (see) the Sphinx, and _____ (climb) up inside one of the pyramids. I _____ (take) a boat up the Nile River, all the way to its source.

PRESENT

Now I _____ (look) for lions as I _____ (ride) through the game reserves. I _____ (take) pictures of the water birds that I _____ (see) on Lake Victoria.

FUTURE

Soon I _____ (stand) at the top of Victoria Falls, where I _____ (feel) the wet spray on my face. I _____ (take) a boat down the Congo River, and I _____ (watch) for crocodiles!

Grammar and Usage Workbook

A TERRIBLE TRIP

Bad News Bentley is telling Birdseye about the time he went to Africa. It was a trip full of bad news from beginning to end.

Fill in the correct past tense or past perfect form of each verb to finish the story.

Last year I _____ (go) to Africa. Everything that I _____ (do) went wrong. I _____ (fight) off mosquitoes every night. I _____ (forget) to take my toothbrush. One day I _____ (bring) a picnic lunch, but a vulture _____ (fly) off with it. Just when I _____ (think) things might be getting better, an elephant _____ (stand) on my suitcase. A baboon had already _____ (break) my umbrella, and a monkey had _____ (steal) my sunglasses. When I _____ (see) that a zebra had _____ (eat) my hat, I _____ (give) up. Well, what would you have _____ (do)? So I _____ (go) to the airport—only to find that the plane had already _____ (leave) without me. Then I _____ (know) I should have stayed home!

Remind me never to travel with Bentley.

Grammar and Usage Workbook

SUMMER STORM

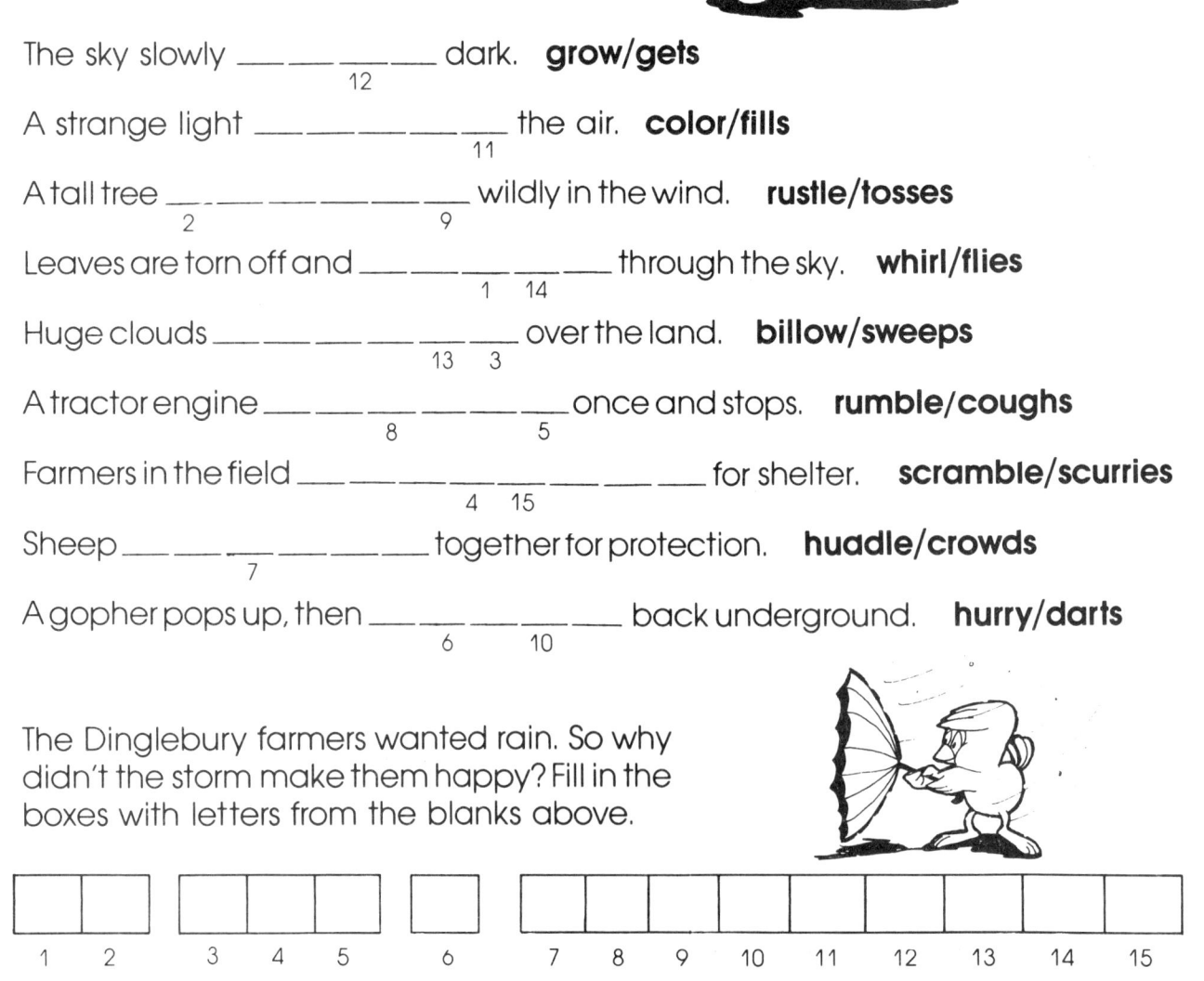

All the farmers in Dinglebury are sad. For weeks, they have been hoping for rain. Finally there was a big storm. It lasted for four hours. But when the storm was over, the farmers were sadder than ever. Why?

Read these sentences about the storm. To fill in the blanks, choose the verb that agrees with the subject of the sentence.

The sky slowly __ __ __ __ dark. **grow/gets**
                    12

A strange light __ __ __ __ __ the air. **color/fills**
                       11

A tall tree __ __ __ __ __ __ wildly in the wind. **rustle/tosses**
              2   9

Leaves are torn off and __ __ __ __ __ through the sky. **whirl/flies**
                          1   14

Huge clouds __ __ __ __ __ __ over the land. **billow/sweeps**
                  13 3

A tractor engine __ __ __ __ __ __ once and stops. **rumble/coughs**
                       8   5

Farmers in the field __ __ __ __ __ __ __ __ for shelter. **scramble/scurries**
                           4   15

Sheep __ __ __ __ __ __ together for protection. **huddle/crowds**
              7

A gopher pops up, then __ __ __ __ __ back underground. **hurry/darts**
                         6   10

The Dinglebury farmers wanted rain. So why didn't the storm make them happy? Fill in the boxes with letters from the blanks above.

1	2	3	4	5	6	7	8	9	10	11	12	13	14	15

8 Grammar and Usage Workbook

SNOW IN THE CITY

Fill in the blanks with wasn't or weren't.

A snowstorm hit the city, and it _____ just a little one. People _____ ready for all that snow. Traffic _____ a problem—because there _____ any! Cars _____ able to make their way through the drifts. Until the streets could be cleared, city buses _____ running. Only the underground subway _____ stopped by the storm.

Fill in the blanks with doesn't or don't.

Birds _____ like winter storms. Bare trees _____ offer much shelter from the wind. The fountain where they drink _____ work—it is frozen solid! And the deep snow _____ make it easy to find things to eat. Someone put sunflower seeds on the windowsill—why _____ some poor bird come and enjoy this feast?

I think I know why not...

Grammar and Usage Workbook

WHO'S AFRAID OF THUNDER?

"Why are you hiding under the bed?"

Read what the fellow under the bed is saying. He is so nervous, he can't remember the rules about negative words. Choose the best word to finish each sentence.

1. It's not because I heard _____ thunder.
   _{no/any}

2. I don't _____ get scared by thunderstorms.
   _{ever/never}

3. I know a little thunder doesn't hurt _____ .
   _{nobody/anybody}

4. I just don't feel like watching _____ lightning.
   _{no/any}

5. I don't like to do _____ in a thunderstorm.
   _{anything/nothing}

6. There isn't anyone to talk to _____ .
   _{anyhow/nohow}

7. It's funny, I haven't seen _____ lightning or heard
   _{no/any}
   _____ rain — only thunder.
   _{no/any}

8. Maybe there wasn't _____ thunder after all.
   _{no/any}

9. Why didn't _____ remind me about noisy
   _{nobody/somebody}
   garbage collectors?

10. I don't want to hear _____ wisecracks from
    _{no/any}
    _____ !
    _{no one/anyone}

10 Grammar and Usage Workbook

CHOCOLATE SOAP?

Max writes advertisements for new products. Some of his slogans appear below, but they are jumbled up. Find the best subject for each predicate, and write it in the blank.

New SCRUB soap is made of real chocolate.
The X-14 sports car will make your teeth clean and white.
Choc-o-chunk candy will keep you cool.
Bright Bite toothpaste will turn you beanstalk into a giant.
Jack's Plant Food is the perfect dessert.
Sticko wallpaper paste never loses its curl.
A Whirly Breeze fan has special power brakes.
Mom's Apple Pie will make your clothes look like new.
A Shaggy Mane wig sticks tighter than glue.

_____ is made of real chocolate.

_____ will make your teeth clean and white.

_____ will keep you cool.

_____ will turn your beanstalk into a giant.

_____ is the perfect dessert.

_____ never loses its curl.

_____ has special power brakes.

_____ will make your clothes look like new.

_____ sticks tighter than glue.

Think of three advertising slogans. Write the subjects and predicates on separate slips of paper, and make your own mixed-up slogans. Have a friend try to straighten them out.

Grammar and Usage Workbook

A CHOICE MEAL

One day Max wrote advertisements for eight different restaurants. He was thinking of food from morning to night.

Underline all the words in the subject of each sentence Max wrote. Then follow the directions below to find out where Max went for dinner.

1. The view is lovely at Mountaintop Inn.
2. The thickest milkshake in the state is at Nate's.
3. Hank's Drive-in has better hot dogs.
4. Breakfast is a treat at the Doughnut Shop.
5. Extra onions and relish make Lucy's hamburgers special.
6. Mario makes the best pizza in town.
7. Dad and Mom should take the whole family to Sam's Bagel Barn.
8. The service is great at Tia's Tacos.

With all those places to choose from, where did Max go to eat? Write the last letter of each underlined subject in the proper blank.

He ___ ___ ___ ___   ___ ___ ___ ___
    1 2 3 4   5 6 7 8

Grammar and Usage Workbook

FIDO'S FAVORITE

Circle the predicate of each sentence below. Then use the numbered letters from the predicates only to fill in the numbered boxes at the bottom of the page. Be sure not to use any letters from the subject part of a sentence.

Max Martin has a job writing tv ads for new products.

He had to write an ad for Fido's Favorite dog food.

Max decided to get some ideas from the product's users.

But Max, a cat lover, didn't even know a dog.

The puzzled writer chewed his pencil and thought.

An hour passed. Poor Max had not written a single word.

A wonderful idea came to him at last.

He grabbed his coat and ran to his car.

Max drove off, whistling happily.

He would soon have a slogan for Fido's Favorite.

Where did Max go to get an idea for his dog food ad?

When Max writes about birdseed, I can give him some ideas.

Grammar and Usage Workbook

EXCITABLE SUSAN

Excitable Susan is telling about something she just saw. Susan is so excited that she forgets to use complete sentences. Rewrite what she says, making complete sentences.

1. A circus monkey on the loose!

2. Crossing the street on a skateboard!

3. Right across to the traffic island.

4. Way up on the traffic light!

5. Hung by one arm.

6. Swinging back and forth.

7. Then on across the street.

8. Leaping from car roof to car roof.

9. Thought it looked so funny!

10. What a goofy monkey!

SURPRISE PACKAGE

Excitable Susan goes on and on. She doesn't even stop to take a breath! Rewrite what Susan is saying. Divide her paragraph into shorter sentences, and add punctuation to make it easier to understand.

When I came home from school there was a package in the mailbox and it wasn't my birthday but my mom said I could open the box and when I did I almost screamed because it was full of bright red ladybugs that were crawling all over each other and who would have sent us bugs so my mom laughed and said they were for the garden but I never heard of anyone getting bugs in the mail this way did you?

Would you mind saying that again?

NOISE IN THE KITCHEN

Read about Excitable Susan's latest excitement. Label each sentence. Write <u>I</u> before every incomplete sentence. Write <u>R</u> before every run-on sentence. Write <u>OK</u> before every sentence that is all right.

1. ____ Everyone was asleep the house was quiet.

   ____ A noise downstairs like soft footsteps.

   ____ Right away, I wondered what it was.

2. ____ Then I quickly grabbed my baseball bat.

   ____ Hurrying, I tiptoed downstairs the noise was in the kitchen.

   ____ Heart pounding, such a brave girl!

3. ____ Ready to pounce, ready to be a hero.

   ____ Finally I rushed into the kitchen.

   ____ Excitable Susan is what they call me I was lucky I didn't swing my bat.

What did Excitable Susan find in the kitchen? Use the first letter of each sentence above to fill in the blanks. Follow the code.

A ham sandwich?

__ __ __   __ __ __ __ __ __ __ __ __
2-I 3-R 1-OK   3-OK 1-I 2-OK 2-R 1-R 3-I

16   Grammar and Usage Workbook

TROUBLE AT THE TREE

Birdseye has been reading ghost stories at night, and now she thinks her tree is haunted. Read what happens one night.

| and | but | or |

Fill in the blanks with the best conjunction to make each sentence into a good compound sentence. When you use <u>or</u>, leave the last blank empty.

1. At midnight, Birdseye is wide awake, ___ ___ ___ every feather is standing on end.
                                       1 2 3

2. She hasn't <u>seen</u> anything, ___ ___ ___ she heard a noise.
                               4 5 6

3. Birdeye knows she didn't make any noise, ___ ___ ___ something did.
                                                 7 8 9

4. Could it be a ghost, ___ ___ ___ is it just the wind?
                          10 11 12

5. A shriek fills the darkness, ___ ___ ___ Birdseye dives under the covers.
                              13 14 15

6. What is it, ___ ___ ___ what is it planning to do?
                16 17 18

7. Birdseye must find out, ___ ___ ___ she will never get any sleep.
                          19 20 21

8. Birdseye can't see in the dark, ___ ___ ___ she knows something is prowling below her nest.
                                 22 23 24

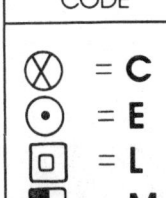

CODE
- ⊗ = C
- ⊙ = E
- ▢ = L
- ◧ = M
- ◓ = S
- ⊞ = Y

WHAT IS HAUNTING BIRDSEYE'S TREE? To find out, use this code and letters from the numbered blanks in the sentences above.

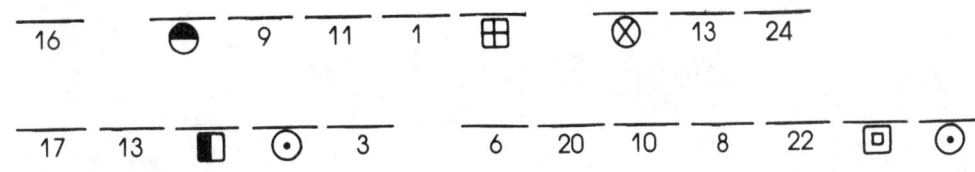

Grammar and Usage Workbook   17

AND . . . AND . . . AND . . .

Birdseye is reading a ghost story called AND . . . AND . . . AND VANISHED! Strangely enough, the word <u>and</u> does not appear until the very end.

Combine each sentence pair into one sentence. Use the word <u>and</u> to make a compound subject or a compound predicate. Write your sentence on the line below each pair.

1. Eric stood in the dark house. His Uncle Lloyd stood there too.

   _____

2. They felt a cold wind. They saw a bluish light.

   _____

3. The light grew brighter. It suddenly went out.

   _____

4. A misty figure swept along the hall. A green glow did too.

   _____

5. The pale figure floated up the stairs. So did the green glow.

   _____

6. The wooden stairs creaked. The stairs groaned.

   _____

7. Then the figure laughed wildly. It vanished.

   _____

8. A strange symbol appeared on the wall. A scrawled message appeared on the wall.

   _____
   _____

This was the message:

Grammar and Usage Workbook

FAMOUS GHOSTS

Words like the ones on this haunted staircase often begin a clause that is joined to another sentence.

(Circle) these words in the sentences below.

Draw a line under the clause they introduce.

1. A ghostly hitchhiker stands at Devil's Curve when the night is dark and rainy.

2. You may see Lincoln's ghost, tall and somber, if you stay late in the White House some night.

3. While riding home late one night, Ichabod Crane was chased by the Headless Horseman.

4. Anne Boleyn has often been seen in the Tower of London since she died there 400 years ago.

5. Movie actress Elke Sommer left her house in Beverly Hills because strange events occurred there.

6. Although the Nameless Horror of London had the shape of a man, its head was that of a beast.

7. The ghostly faces of two sailors followed the S. S. Watertown after the men died at sea.

Grammar and Usage Workbook

HAVING THE COMMAS

Comma Kid, the famous comma collector, is in bed. He has collected all the commas from the sentences below. But he has something else, too. What is it?

Put the commas back where they belong. In the blank before each sentence, write the number of commas you added.

_____ Our friend the Comma Kid has been drinking lemonade orange juice ice water limeade and tomato juice.

_____ He has the sneezes the sniffles and a sore throat.

_____ Now he reaches for his box of tissues which is almost empty.

_____ The thermometer which he just used shows that he has a fever.

_____ Poor Comma Kid has nothing to do but read his junk mail watch tv and stare at the ceiling.

_____ Daisies which are his favorite flower came with a get-well card from Jethro his best friend.

_____ Comma Kid feels tired sick gloomy bored and miserable.

_____ Later if he feels better he will get up get dressed go out and collect some more commas.

What does the Comma Kid have? Following the numbers you wrote, fill in the blanks below with the first letter from the proper sentence.

For me, having the commas is like having chicken pox. Is that what the Comma Kid has?

He has a 'comma' ___ ___ ___ ___ ___
                      1   4 6 5 3

SOCCER SCHEDULE

The Comma Kid has organized a Soccer League. His team, the Colorado Comma Toes, will play nine games this year. The other teams are listed on the schedule below.

Make up the rest of the Comma Toes team schedule. Fill in the dates—month, day, and year. And fill in the place—city and state. Don't forget commas!

OLD WEST SOCCER LEAGUE						
Colorado Comma Toes				19____ schedule		
TEAM PLAYED	DATE			PLACE		
	month	day	year	city		state
Pikes Peak Packers						
Boot Hill Booters						
Rio Grande Rollers						
Boulder Barn Burners						
Laramie Lemon Squeezers						
Moutain Muleskinners						
Ghost Town Gang						

You name the last two teams!

QUALITY QUOTES

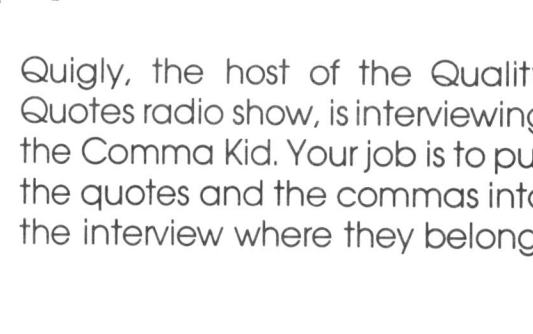

Quigly, the host of the Quality Quotes radio show, is interviewing the Comma Kid. Your job is to put the quotes and the commas into the interview where they belong.

Tell me Kid why do you like commas so much? asked Quigly.

Well Quigly a comma is useful beautiful and a man's best friend said the Comma Kid.

Quigly sputtered But I always thought that man's best friend was a dog.

No a comma is far better than a dog replied the Kid.

Quigly snorted How do you figure that?

Well stated Comma Kid   have you ever heard a comma yelp when you accidently step on its tail?

Do you really mean asked Quigly that you would rather have a comma than a dog for a pet?

Of course answered Comma Kid. A comma never sheds it can be kept in an apartment and it hardly eats a thing.

There you have it folks — a Quality Quote from the Comma Kid. Tune in tomorrow when we will be talking to a Russian wolfhound. Stick around Kid it could be interesting! Quigly finished.

Man's best friend???

ADJECTIVE TROUBLE

"Something's wrong. It must be too cold."

Molly's writing machine has written about a snowy day. The machine is having trouble with adjectives (words that describe). Cross out one adjective in each sentence and write another one above it so the story makes sense.

Snow had fallen all night, and the morning was warm and frosty. Toby and Ella woke up early and looked out at the orange hills.

"The snow is so ugly, I could look at it all day," said Toby.

"Don't just look — let's try out the old sled we got last week," said Ella. The children pulled on their thinnest coats and hurried outside.

Toby and Ella flew down the hills, for the sled was very slow. They threw snowballs and laughed and had a terrible time. They stayed in the snow for hours, until they were rested. Then they went inside for mugs of steaming cold cocoa.

"I love rainy weather," said Toby. "This has been the worst day of the winter."

"It was a dark and sunny night..."

A STICKY PROBLEM

Molly's writing machine is acting up. She asked for a list of adverbs, but the machine dropped in some adjectives, too. Find the **adverbs** in the list, and use them in the story.

quickly	active	young
tired	sadly	smoothly
well	false	funny
carefully	yesterday	loudly

(The clues under the blanks are **opposites**.)

"My writing machine is broken," Molly said _____. It
                                              (happily)
was working _____ yesterday, but now it won't start."
             (badly)
Molly brought out her tools to work on the machine. She took her

time and worked _____. Then she saw the problem.
                  (carelessly)
"No wonder!" she cried _____. "There's a word stuck in
                        (softly)
the machine. It's a word that I put in _____ for a story
                                        (tomorrow)
about my party."

Molly _____ pulled out the word. When she put the
       (slowly)
machine back together, it ran _____.
                               (roughly)

The lesson is, never put a sticky word into a writing machine.

| S | W | T | A | Q | F | L | F | C | S | Y | Y |

In this row of letters, circle the first letter of every adverb you wrote. The letters that are left will be the word that was stuck in Molly's machine.

What is it? ____ ____ ____ ____ ____

24 Grammar and Usage Workbook

SURPRISE!

Molly's writing machine skipped over some of the adjectives and adverbs in this story. Write the correct words in the blanks. Then draw an arrow from each new word to the word it modifies. Remember, adjectives modify nouns and pronouns. Adverbs modify verbs.

Doris planned a _____ party to surprise Molly on
                    wonderful/wonderfully

her birthday. On the day of the party, ten girls

met _____ at Doris's house. All morning, they
      secret/secretly

_____ prepared the food. They made cake and
  busy/busily

lemonade and sticky _____ taffy. Then the girls
                           sweet/sweetly

waited _____ for Molly.
         eager/eagerly

An hour passed. The ice cream melted _____.
                                              slow/slowly

Everyone was very _____. When Doris said, "Let's eat
                         hungry/hungrily

anyway," the girls _____ cut the cake.
                         quick/quickly

Two hours later, Molly _____ came. "I'm sorry," she
                              final/finally

said _____ "I didn't know you were waiting to surprise
      sad/sadly

me."

"The biggest surprise now," said Doris, "is that we left you the

_____ piece of birthday cake."
  last/lastly

_____ birthday,
Happy/Happily
Molly!

Grammar and Usage Workbook 25

GETTING THERE

JOEY THE Jogger is talking about going jogging today. Find and circle every prepositional phrase he uses to describe his route.

I am going...

... where I like.
... from my house.
... by the forest.
... over the hills.
... through the village.
... faster than you.
... steadily onward.
... because it's a nice day.
... under the overpass.

... across the stream.
... into a castle.
... huffing and puffing.
... quite far.
... behind the train depot.
... between the police station and the fire house.
... into my backyard.
... to have sore feet.

Reading from top to bottom, number the circled phrases from 1 to 10. Then, on the map, trace the route Joey has described.

I'm lost already.

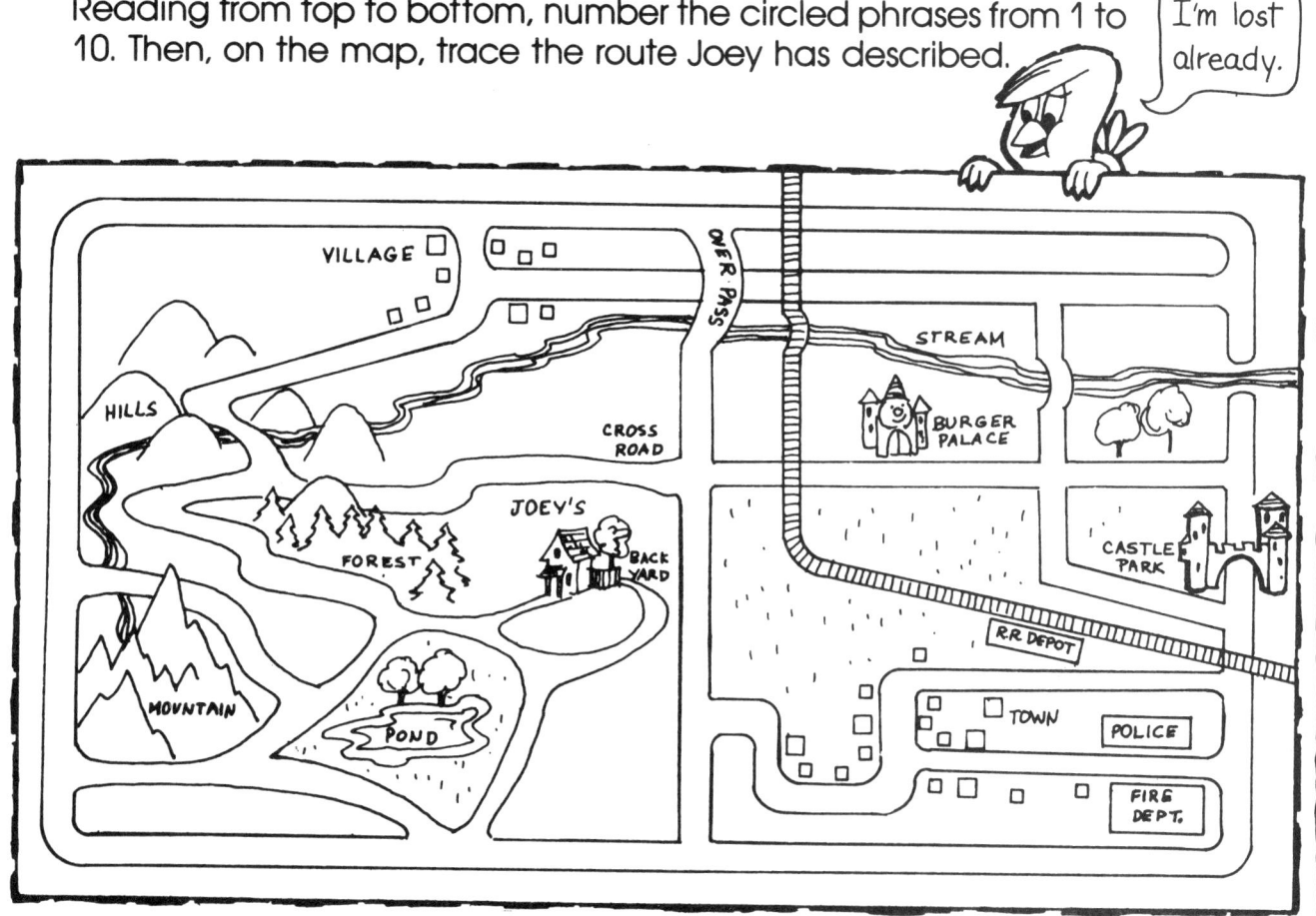

26   Grammar and Usage Workbook

A JOGGER'S PROBLEMS

Finish each sentence with a preposition from the box. Sometimes more than one will fit—just choose one. You may want to use some words more than once.

on	through	for	to
of	by	at	from
in	with	behind	over

Every day last week, Joey the Jogger ran _____ the park.

Every day he had to struggle _____ a new problem.

On Monday, he slipped _____ a banana peel.

On Tuesday, a poodle nipped _____ his heels.

On Wednesday, he stepped _____ a puddle.

On Thursday, he broke one _____ his shoelaces.

On Friday, he was chased _____ a German Shepherd.

On Saturday, he wrote a letter _____ the city park department about making parks safer _____ joggers.

Write your own sentences about Joey the Jogger, using prepositions from the box. Circle the prepositional phrases in your sentences.

_____

_____

_____

_____

_____

Jogging is for the birds!

Grammar and Usage Workbook 27

SEEING THE SOUTHWEST

Cross out the words in parentheses. Replace them with personal pronouns from the box. (You won't use them all.)

| they | me | you | it | we | them | I | he | her | us | she | him |

Maude and Aggie traveled to the southwest United States. First (Maude and Aggie) saw Ship Rock, in New Mexico.

Maude said, "Ship Rock makes (Maude) think of a huge sailing ship. (Maude) could look at (Ship Rock) all day."

Aggie told Maude, "That's silly. How can (Maude) say that looks like a ship?"

SHIP ROCK

Their next stop was at the rocks called Three Sisters. "Who gave (the rocks) that name?" Aggie scoffed. "I have three sisters, but (my sisters) don't look like rocks."

THREE SISTERS

When Aggie saw Window Rock, (Aggie) said, "It's just a rock with a hole in it."

WINDOW ROCK

Finally Aggie saw a sight that (Aggie) liked. Even its name made sense to (Aggie). Aggie sighed, "Why didn't (Maude and Aggie) just come here first?"

Find fourteen personal pronouns in the box, reading from left to right. Circle the pronouns. The letters that are left spell the name of the last place Aggie saw. Write it here:

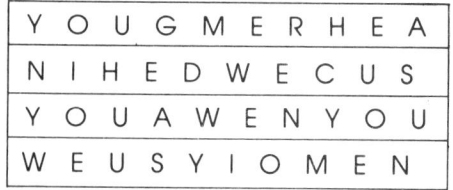

Y	O	U	G	M	E	R	H	E	A
N	I	H	E	D	W	E	C	U	S
Y	O	U	A	W	E	N	Y	O	U
W	E	U	S	Y	I	O	M	E	N

(WEUSYIOMEN?)

_____

28 Grammar and Usage Workbook

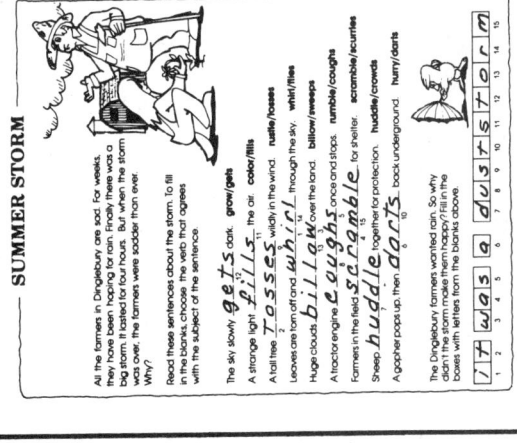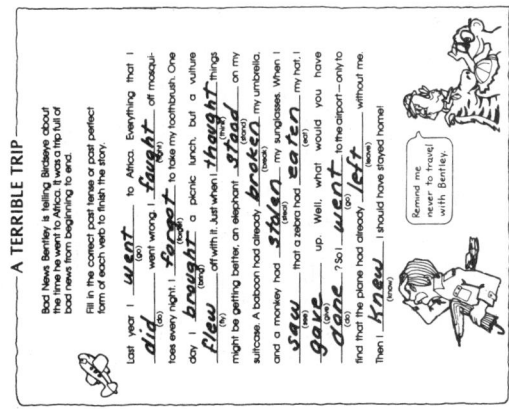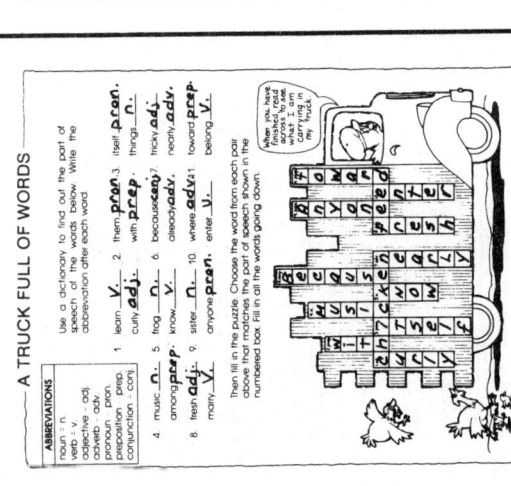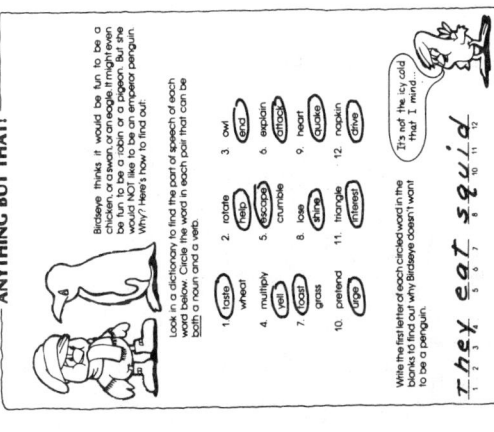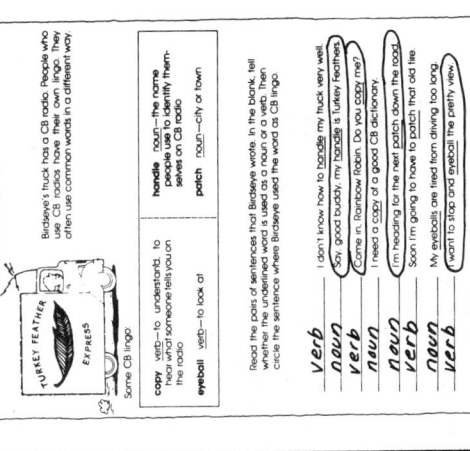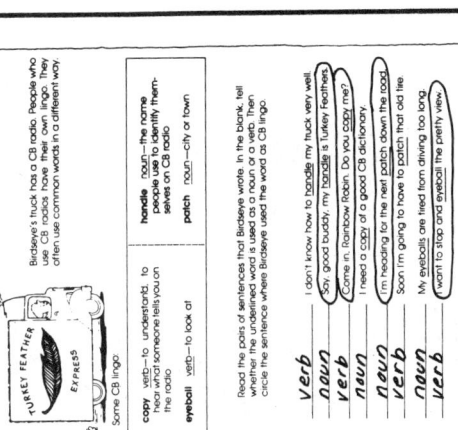

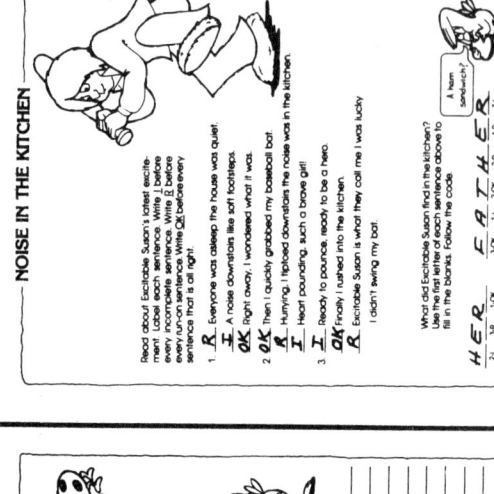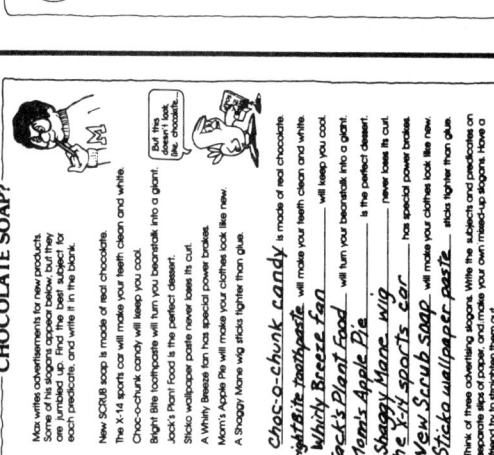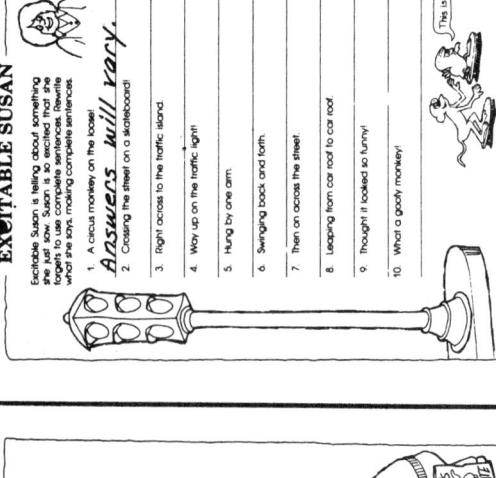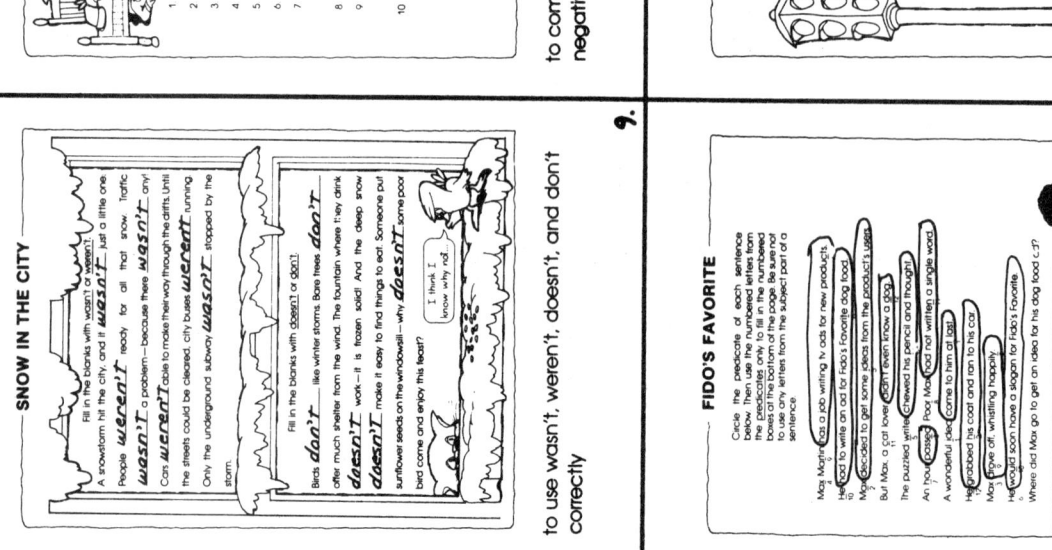

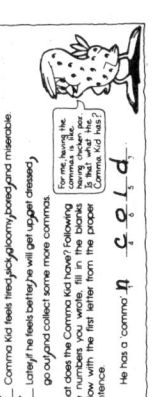
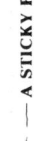
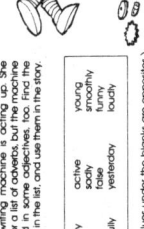
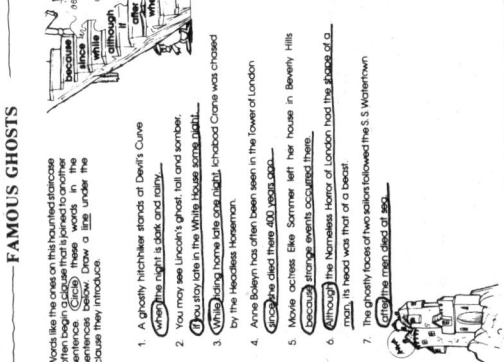

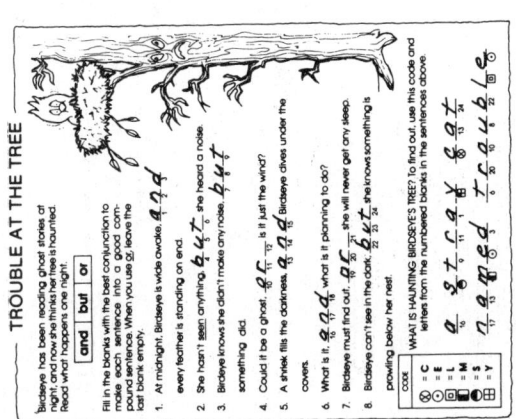

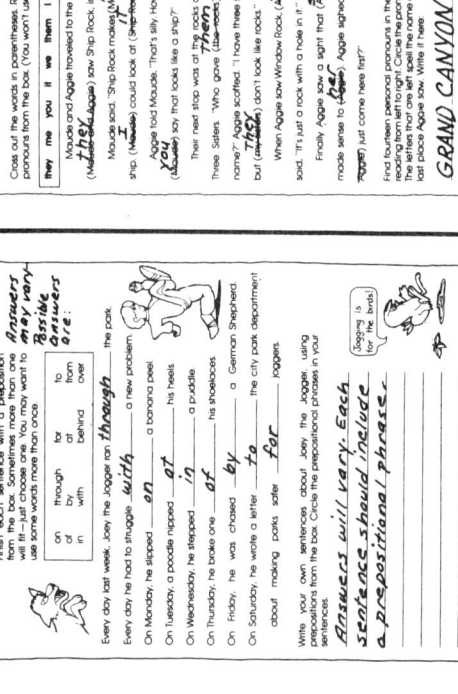

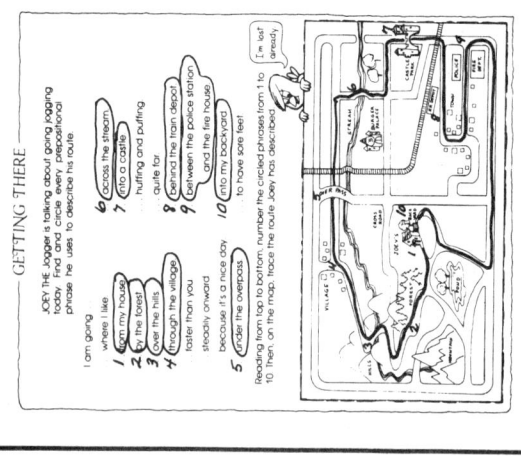

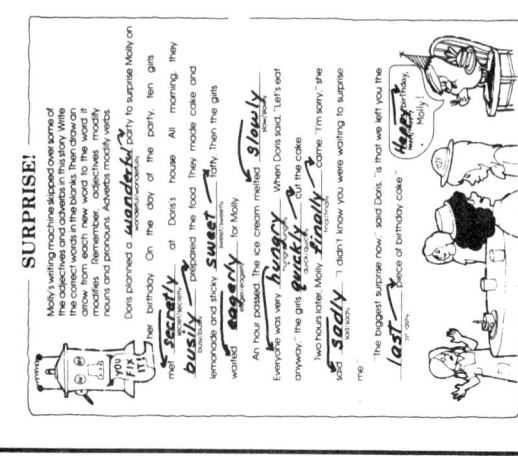